The Dog in the Manger

and other Aesop's Fables

Compiled by Vic Parker

Miles Kelly

First published in 2013 by Miles Kelly Publishing Ltd
Harding's Barn, Bardfield End Green, Thaxted, Essex, CM6 3PX, UK

2 4 6 8 10 9 7 5 3 1

Publishing Director Belinda Gallagher
Creative Director Jo Cowan
Editorial Director Rosie McGuire
Designer Joe Jones
Production Manager Elizabeth Collins
Reprographics Stephan Davis, Jennifer Hunt, Thom Allaway

ISBN 978-1-84810-935-3

Printed in China

British Library Cataloguing-in-Publication Data
A catalogue record for this book is available from the British Library

ACKNOWLEDGMENTS
The publishers would like to thank the following artists who have contributed to this book:
Cover: Tamsin Hinrichsen at Advocate Art
Advocate Art: Natalie Hinrichsen, Tamsin Hinrichsen
The Bright Agency: Marcin Piwowarski
Frank Endersby
Marco Furlotti
Jan Lewis (decorative frames)

Made with paper from a sustainable forest

www.mileskelly.net   info@mileskelly.net

www.factsforprojects.com

Contents

The Wind and the Sun

Once a long time ago, the wind and the sun had an argument about which of them was the strongest.

"I am," said the sun, "for I can burn skin simply by staring at it."

"That may be," said the wind, "but I can toss boats on the waves just by breathing out."

Suddenly they saw below them a traveler on the road. Then the sun had an idea and said, "I see a way to settle this argument. Whichever of us can get that traveler to remove his cloak is the stronger."

The wind went first. He blew upon the
traveler, harder and harder until
trees bent against the
force. But the
traveler just
wrapped his cloak
around him,

holding
on to it
tightly.
At last the wind
gave up. Then the sun
came beaming out and
shone in all her glory

upon the traveler. Immediately, the traveler relaxed his grip on his cloak. Still the sun blazed hotter until the traveler, wiping the sweat from his brow, was forced to take off his cloak entirely.

Kindness can be more effective than harshness.

The Lion, the Fox and the Beasts

The lion once fell ill – so ill that he was sure he was dying. He summoned all the animals to him so he could tell them his last wishes.

First, the goat came to the lion's cave. Trembling, he tottered in. He was gone a long time, so a sheep decided to go in to pay his respects. A calf waiting outside, also decided to enter the cave to hear the lion's last wishes.

After a while, the lion appeared from inside the gloom. Strangely, he was feeling stronger. He saw a fox waiting outside. "Why did you not come to see me?" he snarled.

"I beg your pardon," said the
fox, "but I noticed the tracks
of the animals that had
entered the cave.

And while I see many going in, I can't see any
coming out. Until all the animals that entered
the cave come out, I will stay here."

It is easier to get into an enemy's clutches than to get out again.

8

The Cat-maiden

Long, long ago, in the early days of the world, the great god Zeus ruled over the Earth. This did not stop the other gods and goddesses from arguing with him from time to time.

One day Venus, the goddess of beauty, was debating with Zeus if it was possible for a living thing to change its natural habits and instincts. Zeus said yes, it was – for instance, a camel could stop being bad-tempered if it so wished and be content and good-natured all the time. However, Venus said it was impossible – a camel could not stop being bad-tempered, just as a rabbit could not become fierce like a tiger, nor could a crocodile become vegetarian.

To test the question, Zeus turned a cat into a maiden, and gave her to a young man to take for his wife. The wedding was carried out with much rejoicing and celebration, and the young couple sat down to the wedding feast.

"See," said the mighty Zeus to the beautiful Venus, "how perfectly she behaves. Who could tell that yesterday she was but a cat? Surely her nature is changed?"

"Wait a minute," replied Venus, and with a flick of her fingers, she conjured up a mouse. No sooner did the bride see the mouse than she tried to pounce upon it.

"Ah, you see," said Venus. "You will have to agree that I am right after all!"

The true nature of a living thing will always show itself in the end.

The Lioness
and the
Fox

A lioness and a fox were once talking about their young, as mothers often do, and praising everything about them.

"My children are the picture of health," said the fox, "I have had many compliments on how big and strong they are growing."

"Well, my child has a particularly splendid coat," said the lioness, "and his mane is clearly going to be quite a sight to see once he reaches adulthood."

"Everyone tells me how my children are the image of their parents," said the fox proudly.

"And I am often told that my son is clearly going to be as strong and courageous as his father," insisted the lioness.

"When I see my litter of cubs playing together, it's an absolute joy to behold," said the fox, then she added, rather maliciously, "but I notice you never have more than one."

"That's true," said the lioness with a steely glint in her eye, "but that one grows up to be the King of the Beasts."

Quality, not quantity.

13

The Donkey
and its
Shadow

Long ago, there was a man who wanted to leave his home in the city and move to another, some distance away.

In order to take all his possessions with him, he hired a donkey, for he had too much to carry. He struck a deal with the donkey's owner, who would load the animal, and come on the journey to drive the donkey and feed and water it.

All went well to begin with – the owner arrived with the donkey, and loaded it up. They set off down the road, making good progress until the sun blazed overhead and they were forced to stop and rest.

The traveler wanted to lie down in the donkey's shadow, but the owner wouldn't let him — he said he had hired the donkey, not its shadow. The traveler argued that his bargain gave him control of the donkey... and so the argument went on. The quarrel grew heated, until they came to blows. Of course, while the men were fighting, the donkey took to its heels and was soon out of sight.

If you quarrel about something that is unimportant, you may well lose what is important.

The Hound and the Hare

There was once a young hound who sniffed out a hare and chased her at full speed until he had caught up with her.

The hare was terrified, waiting for death and wondering why the hound did not finish her off. One moment he would lunge at her and snap with his teeth as though he were about to kill her – even grabbing her coat in his jaws. Then the next, he would let her go and leap about playfully, as if having fun with another dog.

The tormented hare grew more desperate until at last she gasped, "I wish you would show your true colours. If you are my friend, why do you bite me? If you are my enemy, why do you play with me?"

Anyone who plays double is not a true friend.

The Dog and the Wolf

It was a hot day on the farm, and the dog was on guard at the gate. He was having trouble staying awake. The

flies were buzzing drowsily, and from the fields came the sound of cows mooing and sheep bleating contentedly. The dog's attention faded. First one eye drooped, then the other. Then, out of nowhere, a wolf pounced! Suddenly, the dog was fighting for his life. He begged for mercy, saying, "Wolf, you see how thin I am? I will make a wretched meal. But if you wait a few days, my master is giving a feast. The leftovers will be mine and I shall get nice and fat. This will be a better time to eat me." So the wolf just snarled and sloped away. As the dog had said, the feast took

place and he ate his fill of tasty leftovers. The next day, the wolf arrived, only to find the dog out of reach on the stable roof.

"My friend," the dog said, "if you catch me down there again, don't wait for any feast."

Once bitten, twice shy.

The Wolf, the Fox and the Ape

There was once a time when a wolf and a fox were firm friends. They went hunting together and shared whatever food they caught between them. However one day, an argument arose between them.

The wolf caught a deer on a mountainside and left it lying on the rocks while he went to drink at a stream. When he returned from quenching his thirst, the body of the deer had vanished – and the fox was lurking nearby. In his fury, the wolf accused the fox of stealing the deer from him – which the fox strongly denied. Each animal accused and insulted the other, and neither would back down. So they agreed to take their argument to someone else to judge.

The wolf and the fox presented their grievances to an ape, who listened carefully to each of them, and then announced, "I do not think that you, dear wolf, ever lost the body of a deer, as you say you did. But all the same I believe that you, dear fox, are guilty of the theft, in spite of all your denials."

The dishonest get no credit, even if they act honestly.

The Lion and the Boar

One hot day, a lion and a boar came to a spring at the same time to drink. They argued as to who should drink first.

"I was here first," growled the boar.

"Not so," insisted the lion, "I arrived seconds before you."

"False!" said the boar.

"You should give way to me," countered

the lion, "as I am King of the Beasts."

The quarrel continued, until the lion and the boar suddenly charged at one another in a frenzy. They fought furiously until, pausing to take a breath, they saw some vultures seated on a rock above. The beady-eyed birds were obviously waiting for one of them to be killed so they could feed upon the dead carcass.

"If you're thinking what I'm thinking," said the lion, "we'd better make up."

"Yes," agreed the boar, "I'd rather forget our quarrel and live, than fight to the death and be food for vultures."

Those who argue and fight may be watched by others, who will take advantage of the loser to do better for themselves.

The Wolf
and the
Lamb

Once upon a time, a wolf was on a hillside, lapping at the cool waters of a spring when, looking up, what should he see but a lamb having a drink a little lower down.

The wolf hadn't eaten for a day or two and the lamb was young and plump. 'There's my supper,' thought the starving wolf, 'and very tasty it looks too. If only I could find some way to get hold of it.'

The wolf stood quietly, watching the lamb splash in the water in the warmth of the sun. His back bristled with temptation and his stomach growled with hunger. He licked his lips and roared out angrily to the lamb, "Hey – you down there! Stop tramping about at the edge of the stream – you are muddying the water from which I am drinking!"

The lamb jumped back in shock at the sight of the wolf. "No, master, no!" he said, all of a tremble. "If the water is muddy up there, it can't be my fault, because it's flowing from you down to me here."

A drop of saliva fell from the wolf's drooling jaws. "Well then," he spat, "why did you call me insulting names this time last year? You know you did!"

"L-l-l-last y-y-y-year?" stammered the lamb, bewildered. "That couldn't have been me – I am only six months old, I wasn't alive last year."

"I don't care," snarled the wolf, "if it wasn't you, it must have been another of your family." And with that, he sprang down the hillside. In just three great bounds he had leapt upon the little lamb and in a few moments he was hungry no longer.

A tyrant will use any reason as a cause for his wickedness.

The Lion's Share

Alion once went hunting with a fox, a jackal and a wolf. The four hunters prowled and lurked and tracked until at last they came upon a huge deer in the depths of a forest. Working together, they took the deer totally unawares and claimed its life.

The hunters stood triumphant as the deer lay before them. But then they all began to wonder how they should share out their catch.

Just as an argument was about to break out, the lion threw back his head and gave a mighty

roar. "Divide this deer up into quarters right NOW!" he bellowed, and the other leapt to it. When it was done, the lion snarled at the fox, the jackal and the wolf, who stood sulkily before him. "The first quarter is for me," he declared, "because I am King of the Beasts."

The fox, the jackal and the wolf looked at each other and shrugged – that was fair enough, they thought. But then the lion went on... "The second quarter is mine too, as I am the one sorting out the shares."

"But—"

"Hang on a minute—"

"Nonsense!" The fox, the jackal and the wolf began to grumble, but the lion took no notice and carried on.

"The third share should be mine because of the part I played in hunting the deer. As for the fourth quarter, well, I should like to see which of you will dare to lay a paw upon it." And the lion bared his teeth and flexed his sharp claws.

The three other hunters slunk away into the shadows with their tails between their legs.

Powerful people are more than happy to let you do some of their work, but they won't share the rewards.

The Fox
and the
Monkey

A fox and a monkey were once travelling together. They were chatting to pass the time, when they fell into an argument about which of them was the more noble creature.

"Of course, of the two of us, I am the grandest animal," said the fox. "I come from a line of brave and highly respected hunters."

"Surely I am the more noble of us," insisted the monkey, "for my family live high above yours, in the trees."

On and on they went, bickering away for quite some time, until they passed a cemetery. The cemetery was full of grand, beautifully carved monuments to the dead buried there.

The monkey looked around and fell quiet for a moment or two, thinking. Then he let out a big sigh.

"What on earth has made you sigh like that?" asked the fox.

The monkey pointed to the huge, expensive tombs all around and replied, "All the monuments that you see here were put up in honour of my fathers and my fathers' fathers, who in their day were very important."

The fox was speechless for a moment, but quickly recovered and said, "Oh! Please keep on with your lies – don't stop now. You're quite safe, no matter what ridiculous claims you make, because none of these poor souls can rise up and say that you're talking absolute rubbish!"

Boasters show off the most when no one can prove that they are lying.

The Dog
in the
Manger

There was once a dog who was looking for a nice, warm place to take an afternoon nap. The horse was in the shade under the tree. The hen was curled up in the cart. The cat was basking in the sun on the barn roof.

The dog slunk into the barn and looked for a spot that was not yet taken. Suddenly his eyes came to rest on the ox's manger. It was filled with fresh, sweet-smelling hay. 'That's the place for me,' thought the dog, and he trotted over, jumped in and settled down to sleep.

A little later, the
ox plodded into
the barn. He
was hot and tired
from ploughing all
day. After drinking at
the water trough he
went to his manger to
eat, and found the
dog fast asleep!

The ox's hot breath roused the dog from his dreams, and he jumped up, snarling. Each time the ox came near to try to take a mouthful of hay, the dog tried to bite him, even though he did not want to eat the hay himself. At last the ox was forced to give up and go away hungry.

People may not want others to have things, even if they can't use them themselves.

The Goat and the Vine

A goat wandered into a vineyard one day, where the vines grew strong and thick, and were dripping with the juiciest grapes. She couldn't believe her luck at having stumbled upon such a delicious treat, and at once trotted over to the nearest stems and began to graze on the tender green shoots.

All of a sudden, the goat heard a voice moaning. She looked all around but no one was near. Then she realized with a start that it was the vine itself.

"Whatever have I done to you for you to hurt me like this?" it sobbed. "Isn't there enough grass for you to feed on?"

Before the goat could reply, the vine said,
"But even if you eat every leaf and leave me
bare, I will still produce wine for the cook to add
to the pot when you are being cooked as a stew."

If you cross somebody, you
can be certain they will want
to get their own back.